MY YELLOW
HEART

poems

Cover art by Vi Khi Nao
Cover design by Diana Le

First Edition
Published by Girl Noise Press
girlnoise.net

ALSO BY VI KHI NAO

The Vanishing Point of Desire (2015)

Fish In Exile (2016)

The Old Philosopher (2016)

Umbilical Hospital (2017)

A Brief Alphabet of Torture (2017)

Sheep Machine (2018)

The Vegas Dilemma (2021)

A Bell Curve Is A Pregnant Straight Line (2021)

Swimming With Dead Stars (2022)

Waiting For God (2022)

Fish Carcass (2022)

MY YELLOW HEART

poems

VI KHI NAO

GIRL NOISE

PRESS

CONTENTS

I.

II.

33 YOU ARE NOT A LOAF OF BREAD THAT THE NIGHT
   MUST FORGIVE IN ORDER TO BE VIOLENT

34 I'M GOING TO HOLD YOUR MONEY HOSTAGE IF YOU
   ARE NOT NICE TO ME & ACCOMMODATIONS ARE 2X
   $$ DURING XMAS

35 IF YOU MUST BEG, DO NOT WEAR THE SAME
   GARMENT AS THE FUTURE

36 LICK MY EYELID BEFORE YOU GO, SAY YOUR ORGANS
   ARE LONELY, RUB MY HIP STUDIOUSLY, COMB MY
   HAIR NOW TO AVOID PATROL, HAVE MY LIVER
   FOR LIFE

37 THE ECONOMY OF YOUR DESIRE HAS ENTERED THE
   ICE AGE OVERNIGHT, FROZEN LAKES OF DESPAIR, IT
   WILL TAKE FOREVER TO THAW OUT YOUR HAIR,
   EXOGENOUS ZONES, THE EVERGLADES OF YOUR
   TONGUE & FINGER MORTGAGES, THE
   UNEMPLOYMENT BENEFITS OF OUR KISSES HAVE
   PLUNGED INTO 26 MILLION, THERE ARE BILLIONS
   OF STIMULATIONS, BUT NONE COULD GET THE DICK
   HARD, ENOUGH TO KICK THE DEPRESSION AWAY

39 MY ROOT IS NOT A MIRROR, WHICH HAS THE FACE
   OF GLASS, MY ROOT ISN'T AN ORCHID, NOT
   WATERED IN A WEEK

40 I CAN'T HURRY TIME FOR YOU OR TIE IT TO A
   DOORKNOB TO STRETCH IT OUT LIKE A RUBBER
   BAND TO ONE'S TONGUE OR TO PLACE IT ON A
   PLATTER OF SMOKE

INDOORS AND CLOSE THE CURTAINS — OF COURSE,
OF COURSE — THEY ARE SYLPH BEINGS ANCHORED
BY DEVASTATION & LUMINESCENCE

51   IN LIFE I AM LED TO NOWHERE BY THE LEFT HAND
OF YOUR HOPE & IN DEATH I IMAGINE ALL THE
POSSIBILITIES: YOU GETTING INTO A HEAD-ON
COLLISION WITH DESTINY & YOUR SEMI
JACK-KNIFED BY THE INSECURITIES AND DOUBTS
THAT LED US ASTRAY

52   MY BABY IS IN MY BED & SEXY & MY BABY, WHOSE
TIT IS EVERGREEN, IS HICCUPING ON MY STOVE
WHILE I AM RAINING RADISH INTO YOUR SKI BOOT
& IT'S YESTERDAY'S AFTERNOON WHILE HER
ORANGE FEATHER IS BOUND BY RUBBER NEAR A
FLORAL OF SOYBEANS

53   I WANT YOUR BRIEF ESCARPMENT HIGHLIGHTING A
YOUTHFUL PERFECTION, ITS DAILY TASK, AND I
WANT A DOOR TO EMBODY MY SPIRITUAL BOTTOM

54   I GAZE AT MY NONSELF, KNOWING THAT I HAVEN'T
EXISTED YET, BUT IN YOU MY OTHER SELF REVEALS
ITS METAL AMALGAM, IT REVEALS THAT I AM NOT
YOU, I AM A DISTORTED FRAGMENT OF SOMETHING
SOFT IN THE PERIPHERY

55   I TOOK A NAP ON AN ELECTRIC CHAIR AND
CONFUSED IT FOR A FLOCK OF PRIVATE
ELECTROCUTION AS SUCH THERE IS A DEER IN MY
RED EARTH PAST, BOWING HER HEAD SIMILARLY TO
A BLACK AND WHITE ÁO DÀI

ACKNOWLEDGMENTS

Early versions of these poems appeared somewhere there. The poet wishes to thank the following editors and their respective journals:

Maya Marshall @ *Underbelly*; Cynthia Bargar @ *Pangyrus*, Evan Isoline @ *Selffuck*; Andrew Wessels, Avni Vyas, Nik De Dominic @ *The Offending Adam*; Em J Parsley & Kelly Andrews @ *Pretty Owl Poetry*; Morgan Vo @ *GLOSS*; Andrew Felsher & Yehui Zhao @ *128 Lit*; Steve Barbaro @ *New Sinews*

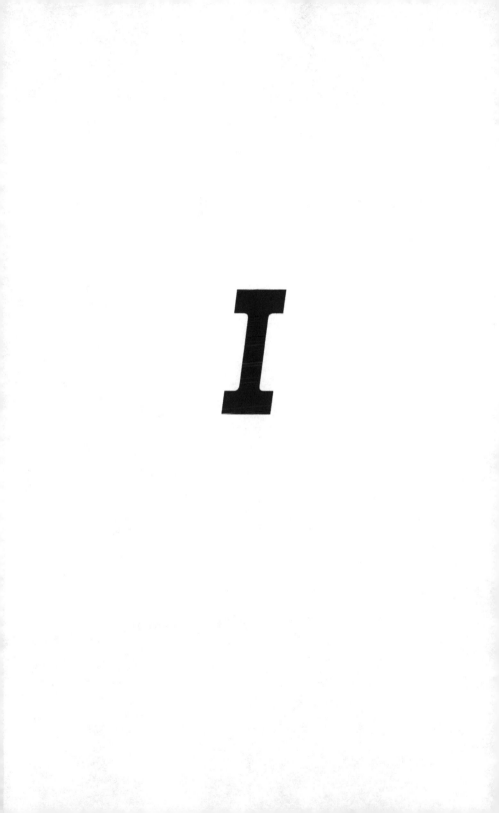

I

ECLIPSE/ECLIPSE AND THE LIGHT BETWEEN

FROM: Erik Ehn   Wed, Mar 23, 12:00 PM
BCC: me
SUBJECT: an upcoming invitational. come on aboard!
BODY:

Eclipse/Eclipse and the Light Between

This spring there's a solar eclipse on 4/30/22, followed by a lunar eclipse a couple of weeks later on 5/15/22 (or 5/16, depending on time zone).

Friend Rae Diamond offers—

> the idea of eclipses as interruptions/interference
> in the cyclical experience of light on Earth...
> light being a metaphor for awareness and understanding.
> Eclipse windows are times when, having a break
> from our usual cycles of thought, some new way of
> understanding
> and experiencing ourselves/everything-else can emerge.
> Deepening commitment to one's true values
> engenders beneficial metamorphosis.

Let's do that, then.

Here's a collective exercise:
Commit two weeks to compassionate noting. In particular, note changes. This is in support of a theme:

Changed-for-Changing

We allow the acute, the keen in us, that which we use to reach and touch (to nurse, to prosecute) to magnify and change us into more and more alert change agents, that we may know better how to be of use to anti-wars. This activity includes the proposition that reaching itself is useful, in that it is charged with life, and the future we desire is as full of desire for us, in the present, fully alive.

Eclipse and eclipse are parentheses around vivid attention. We engage with the two-week interim as a lamp for finding, firming, bearing witness.

Form:
Render the changes you note as zuihitsu—lists built to cause surprise through a mix of surprise and variety.

Send these lists in (one a day? one overall? it is possible to have a list of one... or none) by May 17. I'll compile them and recirculate.

Lists to build an archive against erasure. Lists to avow change remains possible despite static fascism expressed wherever property is asserted over process. Lists to serve the promise art made in us to make us, us.

Let me know if you have questions. Let me know if you'll be jumping in. More news as it breaks.

Peace,
E

SATURDAY: APRIL 30, 2022: 10AM

1. No one uses duct tape as well as my brother.
2. As an Uber driver, my brother drives a white Nissan.
3. When my youngest sister sold the car to him a few years ago, it was in perfect condition.
4. A few nocturnal engagements with a couple of deer and minor accidents led the car to its current demise. Using white duct tape, my brother tapes the front fender and back fender.
5. He layered the tape like a bricklayer, one after the other until the back of his car looks like a brick wall made of duct tape.
6. It's all very symmetrical and organized.
7. He just simply didn't duct tape it in a disorganized, haphazard fashion.
8. No, my brother took his time with the white duct tape.
9. Muck, sprays of mud from rain and snow, and dust coated his white duct taped car, and now it looks more or less like a white football jersey soiled in a thin coat of fine-grained earthy clay.
10. When he picked me up from the airport in Des Moines, it pained me.
11. To see his Uber car in its tattered state.
12. I vowed to use some of the money I won from a recent contest to help him get his new car.
13. My brother is sensitive and self-conscious.
14. Ever since he gained over three or four scores worth of weight, he has been hyper-vigilant about how others treat him.
15. And, little to big things injure him.
16. I should know.

17. I am that way too.
18. I figured the best way to give him money is to give it to him through Ubering me.
19. I rationalized that each time he Ubered me, I paid him.
20. So that when I give him some of the money for the new car, he doesn't feel indebted to me.
21. Ubering gets expensive when it comes to car maintenance.
22. Our garage looks like an auto mechanic shop.
23. There are stacks of car tires lining the walls of our garage.
24. Ubering punishes the car so severely.
25. My brother is always doing oil changes on it.
26. Is always rotating his tires.
27. I felt almost proud of myself for being so permeable about this.
28. I counted my eggs too early.
29. So when my youngest sister texted me the following message, "Vi, your brother is not coming because you keep Venmo-ing him for silly things so it'll be just us."
30. I grew sad all over.
31. Even when I Zoomed with my partner while she was in Little Rock grieving the death of her brother a year ago, tears kept on falling and falling and falling like elderberry liquor from a fast.
32. The French liked to climb the mountain to collect elderberry flowers, but I seem to climb mountains made of razor blades no matter what kind of boots I wear to protect my heart from pain.
33. I wanted my youngest sister and I and my brother to eat together. It has been so long since I saw all of them.

34. Most of the time, I was in Lafayette teaching CU Boulder students and I missed my brother massively.
35. And so I cried because it would just be me and my youngest sister.

SUNDAY MAY 1, 2022

1. My brother is giving my youngest sister tips on dining.
2. He asks her to tip the sushi chefs $10.
3. To drop it into a translucent vessel that looks like a fishbowl.
4. The dollar, like a green minnow, swims lifelessly inside it.
5. Due to my brother's generous tip and insider information about dining at Asian restaurants, the chef immediately bestows upon us a sushi dish of seaweed and white fish, on the house, while we wait for our shrimp tempura and Hawaiian rolls.
6. My brother kept on winking at my youngest sister and she tried to dodge his wink by saying, "I get it now. I get it now."
7. She had, miraculously, convinced him to dine with us despite his resistance a day ago.
8. Her persuasion lightened my heart, reversed my small river of tears, and my chest stopped throbbing in pain.
9. I folded my brother's laundry this late Sunday afternoon.
10. His pants kept on getting bigger and bigger.
11. So did his boxers.

MONDAY MAY 2, 2022

1. My brother is craving hủ tiếu.
2. My younger sister, who is a hairdresser, agrees that she would sell her second pressure cooker to my partner, Jess, and I for 70 dollars.
3. I think it's an awesome deal.
4. My younger sister, the hairdresser, will make hủ tiếu for us all, but especially for my brother.
5. After sleeping for 12 hours, I feel completely wiped out.
6. From the sectional sofa, I could see my brother taking a plate up to his room.
7. It's a plate filled with mandarin oranges.
8. From my view, it almost seems as if he is carrying one orange planet and their two orange moons up into his room.
9. He sleeps as much as I do.
10. 14 hours or more a day.

1. My father flew to Vietnam in order to have sex freely with prostitutes without his wife (whom he brought over from Vietnam to work in a nail shop in the United States) berating him constantly for his concupiscent appetite.
2. My father is lonely.
3. My brother, on the other hand, has become a surrogate father for my youngest brother, the one whom my youngest sister invited over to her new house, in which he turns his penis into a hose and sprays her new bathroom with urine.
4. He peed all over the toilet, all over the bathroom sink, all over the floor.
5. My youngest sister made him get on his hands and knees and clean it.
6. She won't tolerate misogynistic vandalization from a Viet boy who is only six years old.
7. But, his violent and potentially scatological, nitrogen compounded behavior is telling of the abuse he experiences at home.
8. His mother whips him, pinches him, and attacks him whenever she gets the opportunity.
9. Without my father's intermittent, recreational protection, what will happen to this urine-inducing half-brother of mine as my father spends the next three months in Vietnam for casual tourism, prostitution, and dental work?
10. One day, my father, because he can be impatient — aren't we all? — decided to have all of his teeth pulled in Vietnam.
11. Because it's 1/3, 1/2, 1/4? cheaper?

12. As a result, during COVID, while they murdered his gums with metal implants, he only ate soup and smoothies for two years straight.
13. That is true suffering.
14. Devastating suffering.
15. So much of food enjoying (wisdom acquired from my brother) is born from chewing, biting, masticating, manducating, triturating—not from swallowing.
16. It goes without saying: he spent over $300 on a smoothie making machine to ease his gastronomical sorrow.

WEDNESDAY MAY 4, 2022

1. My father pulls the strings of my brother's heart by telling him that when he dies, 1/5 of his current house and his money would go to him.
2. My brother, predicting that he won't lead a long life, asks if he could have his share of the inheritance early.
3. My father, in few words, denies his request.
4. My brother suspects that my father would easily outlive him.
5. I would take the retirement penalty for withdrawing early and give that money to my brother, but he wouldn't accept this gift from me.
6. Today my brother refunded the money I paid for Ubering me home from Des Moines.
7. If he couldn't accept my $200, how was he going to accept 8K?
8. My sister, when driving me through the cornfields to her new house, suspects that my brother endures his pain alone and quietly.
9. Not telling us of the seven years of AFib hardship.
10. She says that his virtue is his downfall.
11. The fact is when he was young, my father used to transport my brother through Saigon as he stood on the motorbike without a single word of complaint while my father drove. Says a lot about his reticent high endurance for pain.
12. I think about my brother a lot.
13. How we, my youngest sister and I, wish he had spoken up sooner.
14. Of his heart pain.

15. Especially when I saw him this morning carrying the coffee he brewed to his broken-down Toyota to make his Uber car smell good for his passengers.

16. Standing inbetween the liminal light, between the garage door and the outside world, he tells me that packages have arrived.

17. My partner's mother has gifted us a white duck comforter.

18. The best kind.

THURSDAY MAY 5, 2022

1. My brother and I are in a small, private competition to see who will die sooner.
2. After three days, my brother ate the shrimp fried rice that we bought for him when we went out to eat at Thai Spice.
3. It made me so happy.
4. We make food for my brother, but the food sits in the refrigerator, senescing, aging without his touch, hunger, or tenderness.
5. He is always on the verge of taking on a diet whenever I prepare food for him.
6. Broccoli and sauteed beef.
7. Baked potatoes and carrots macerated in olive oil and salt.
8. Overboiled corncobs.
9. I wasn't paying attention.
10. The steam smoked rolls and rolls of cigarette on our kitchen stove and counter.
11. Everything I get for him is fresh.
12. But he has a way of diminishing that freshness by letting things rot in the refrigerator before taking bites of it.
13. My brother woke up late and was late to collect his younger stepbrother.
14. It continues to rain, cold rain electrifies the air and prunes my heartbeats.
15. My brother slept into the late afternoon.
16. Both my brother and I are also in competition to see who can sleep the most.
17. I invited my brother to go see the new Dr. Strange with me and my partner.

18. The multiverse kind.
19. His silence empties all the other silences.
20. In our family group text, my brother sends screenshots of lawbreaking Asians.
21. It reads: "*Former treasurer for Iowa City Pride arrested for misuse of funds.*"
22. About $35,732.32, it reads.
23. That seems precise to me.
24. Even to the last two decimal points.
25. They should remove the word "about" from that article.
26. Yesterday, the screenshot he sent us was a Viet "mom accused of shooting sons as they slept — then turning gun on good Samaritan."
27. Her name was Trinh T. Nguyen, 38 years old, of Upper Makefield Township, charged with critically wounding her sons.

1. My brother group texted us a meme of a Prius with the entire front end held together with duct tape that said "My car after 3 years at Lyft."
2. That seems like an accurate portrait of his car and its current condition.
3. My partner and I invited him to see the new multiverse Dr. Strange with us, but he declined.
4. Even though the movie only costs $6 and comes with free tasty, salty popcorn.
5. My brother, shy and self-conscious.
6. I tried to find a million different ways to spend time with him.
7. Each lunch or dinner is declined.
8. Time is not on his side or on mine.
9. The weather has been rain-torn, wet like Portland-Seattle cold, and I am tired and sleepy all the time.
10. With my youngest sister also declining movies with us, I spend time with her whenever she goes to Costco.
11. To get gas.
12. To get groceries.
13. I invite my partner along.
14. My brother shows his love for me by taking out the trash.
15. Keeping the kitchen and bathrooms clean and tidy even though messiness and disorganization are his preferred vernacular or street talk.
16. I don't want him to ever move out.
17. It's wonderful to have him here even though he bestows his ghost to keep us company.

18. At five in the morning, I hear his soft footfalls, his footsteps echoing as he climbs the short stairs into his room.

19. He has returned from Ubering or Lyfting others, nurses who may be getting home from the hospitals or folks starting their early mornings at the office.

20. I want to clean his room for him, without invading his privacy.

21. I want to lower the content of his dust.

22. I want to air his sheets.

23. I want him to know that I care about him.

24. Shall I invade his privacy by cleaning his room for him?

SATURDAY MAY 7, 2022

1. My younger sister, who traveled from her home two hours away, made hủ tiếu for all of us.
2. Her husband carried the big hủ tiếu aluminum pot the size of a thùng phuy into my youngest sister's new home.
3. The shrimp smell was hard on my nose, but it was nice to have an alternate dish, different from her usual, signature dishes: bún riêu and bún bò Huế.
4. My brother drove us over from our home on Court to her home near the new development.
5. There was one huge light beige stone sitting squarely on her yard.
6. It's hard for the man she hired to mow around it.
7. My brother tried to play chess at the same time on his phone while playing tiến lên, Vietnamese poker.
8. His opponent is a real person on the other end.
9. My sister scolded him and he stopped playing chess.
10. He wanted to care less about the game so that he would win.
11. When you stop caring, being detached, things have a way of manifesting for you.
12. Or so I have learned.
13. I discover very quickly that my brother loves peeling and eating gold nugget mandarins.
14. Their skin falls off like orange juice over a rock.
15. Sitting on my youngest sister's deck, my brother observes that her deck is too small.
16. It should wrap itself around the house like a winter blanket.

17. Her backyard is a short-sleeve wearing girl—her bikini is exposed, her skirt is too short, her sandals are laceless.

18. Inside, my nephew, niece, and I unbox these Target chairs.

19. The gray chairs she gave me were prettier.

20. Certain kinds of change aren't always beautiful.

21. My nephew and niece both played video games on their iPads too loud.

22. It drove both my sister and I crazy.

23. We are sensitive to sound.

24. On the way home, my brother observed that the Taco Bell had a long line.

25. Sitting in his backseat like an Uber passenger with an iPad lighting my face like a firefly, I thought that my brother was an amazing driver, of the same extraordinary caliber as the driver in Ryusuke Hamaguchi's recent film *Drive My Car*.

26. The ride home through the cornfields and highways was smooth and unrocky like being inside of a broken boat when the storm has passed.

27. I wanted to give my brother money for gas with gas prices skyrocketing to $4.23.

28. Everything has become so inflated, so expensive now.

29. The roundtrip cost to fly me to Wyoming from Iowa had become $1200.

30. In the past, I could buy three or four roundtrip flights with that amount.

SUNDAY MAY 8TH, 2022

1. At 8:46 am, my brother texted me, "Vi you up?"
2. I called him and we soon headed over to my youngest sister's place for more hủ tiếu.
3. I was craving fried tilapia and my middle sister baked it in her portable air fryer for all of us.
4. The fish was slightly burnt, but its inside was still soft, almost buttery soft.
5. Yesterday, my youngest sister made fish sauce with eight limes for me, but I forgot to bring it home.
6. Today I didn't forget to.
7. Over hủ tiếu and fried tilapia dipped in fish sauce, my middle sister observed that perhaps with my life expectancy diminishing greatly, I won't be able to enjoy the luxury that is coming my way.
8. My youngest sister suspected that I have internal bleeding.
9. My brother suspects that I am bleeding a little each day.
10. They were trying to figure out why I was tired all the time.
11. Yet, if death is just a doorstep away, perhaps I might die before him and before my mother.
12. Perhaps I will be the first one in my family to die.
13. My father already lost seven of his siblings.
14. There were only three left and one has Alzheimer's, which is a type of death of memory in itself.
15. The crypto crash continues to unravel.
16. The stock market is also red like the Red Sea.
17. For Mother's Day, I called my mother and sent her 1000 CRO.
18. CRO's value has declined by half.

19. I purchased 1000 CRO for $500 a month or so ago and now for 1000 CRO, $259.
20. There were wet, heavy tears in my mother's voice.
21. I am aware that my mother is sad and in pain and alone.
22. She spent Mother's Day sad and by herself, in a condo she is deeply allergic to.
23. My brother tries to diminish her sadness by talking to her longer while we played a second session of Vietnamese poker.
24. He knows that she has lost so much money by putting it all on Sofi.
25. Sofi continues to spam my email nonstop.
26. The worst thing I could do for myself is to open an app with them.
27. Meanwhile, my partner is in Kansas City, at this fancy boutique hotel, at her friend's wedding.
28. After the wedding, she would head to Little Rock and Lafayette to end her apartment lease.
29. It was in the morning, a 10am poker game.
30. Poker makes time fly like a horse.
31. My brother and I lost playing Vietnamese poker, with my sisters.
32. We each lost $40.
33. Money I was hoping to make in order to buy the Instant Pot for our new home.
34. My brother was at a McDonald's when my middle sister and her husband came over to help me move the table upstairs.
35. It would be my new drawing desk.
36. While driving us back home from my youngest sister's place, my brother observed, "No one can make money now. Everything is going up and up."

MONDAY MAY 9 2022

1. My middle sister drove over to collect plastic food containers for the hủ tiếu leftovers.
2. To discourage her from making lots and lots more in the future, my youngest sister informed my middle sister that she preferred the bún riêu and bún bò Huế.
3. I thought it was wise.
4. Regardless of what my youngest sister makes, my brother is open to everything.
5. There isn't much in terms of Viet food that he doesn't like.
6. Though there are two cucumbers sitting, rotting in the refrigerator.
7. I was going to prepare us some, but I remember now, last spring, when I was making a cucumber salad, how my brother says he doesn't like cucumbers very much.
8. Having known him for over 40 years, his taste and preferences still surprise me.
9. Continue to surprise me.
10. My youngest sister continues to linger in our kitchen, and I want to ask her what is delaying her or provoking her hesitancy.
11. There was something she wanted to impart.
12. She kept on thanking me for helping her with the chairs, but this repetitive gratitude was a code word, a substitute for something she wanted to impart.
13. I couldn't pull it out of her and she thanked me again as I closed our garage doors.
14. Later, at 1am, when I climbed downstairs to pour more water to drink down my sotalol, I found my brother in the living room, lying on the carpet.

15. His stomach protruded under his black T-shirt like a Buddha.
16. I wonder why he is up so late.
17. I know he prefers sleeping on the floor more than the bed.
18. I know he prefers to straighten his back.
19. My sister from two hours away is shopping for an air fryer for us.
20. She is sending me pictures of industrial blenders for sale at $45.
21. If the owner uses it only once, I imagine us using it less.
22. We have three blenders already.
23. With the recession and inflation, it's a bad time to buy things that will only accumulate dust.
24. Less is less: more is more: less isn't more and more isn't less.
25. I WhatsApped my best friend and she said, "Why do you look so dead tired!"
26. She was extremely frustrated with me.

TUESDAY MAY 10, 2022

1. It's in the 80s, temperature wise, in Iowa City.
2. I understand why my brother is downstairs.
3. It's a lot colder in the living room and heat rises to the top.
4. I find myself sweating for the very first time in a very long time.
5. I open our bedroom window and the crickets are playing their private operas with their whiskers.
6. With the broken dishwasher, I have been handwashing all of our glasses, plates, and dishes.
7. I watched the Hollywood racism documentary on HBO called *Yellowface*.
8. Marlon Brando plays an Asian character in *Sayonara*.
9. Sixty-five years later, history doesn't change very much, remains the same.
10. White men continue to dominate, impolitely, the politics of cinema.
11. I wanted to invite my brother to see a movie tonight.
12. It's Tuesday: free popcorn and $6 movie.
13. But fearing that he may say no, I don't ask.
14. I am on a long phone call with my mother about Sofi.
15. All the stock exchanges such as WeBull, Robinhood, and Ameritrade have halted their trading.
16. The stock price of Sofi continues to fall and fall.
17. It has fallen from over $26 to a little under $5.
18. Sofi's stadium in California ($5.1 billion) is worth more than their stock market cap ($4.9 or so billion).
19. This can't be right.
20. It probably has to do with height: short.
21. Or shorting. Or is it naked shares?
22. My brother sympathizes with my mother.

23. When her stock investment falls, he feels her pain.
24. A chronic gambler himself, he understands fiscal loss.
25. I hear my mother say, "If the boat is small, the wind is also small."
26. My brother, my mother, and I all have small boats.
27. Sometimes they rock us to sleep at night.
28. But most of the time, they give us splinters.
29. Small slivers of wood make their way into our bloodstreams, killing us or giving us pain that goes beyond annoyance.

1. I found my brother lying on the carpet floor in the living room.
2. Not reclining on the sofa nor the other long semi L-shaped sofa.
3. The humidity level is high, at 50% or more.
4. And,the temperature has risen to 90+ degrees.
5. I am sweating for the very first time in five years.
6. I kept on texting my brother over and over again asking if the heat has gotten to him.
7. He texted me back with the following message: Hey just closed the vents in your room if you are cold.
8. He kept on asking if I need a ride to my doctor's appointment tomorrow.
9. I said yes and yes and yes.
10. He is the fastest and closest Uber driver in the Iowa City area.
11. He is because he lives in the bedroom near the guest room of our house.
12. I spend most of today observing the Death Spiral of Terra (LUNA).
13. It went from being worth nearly $120 per LUNA to less than 1 cent.
14. For his arrogance and for taunting everyone for being poor, gamblers are out for his blood.
15. And his wife's blood.
16. Lunatics, fanatic crypto investors of Luna, talk of suicide and then some even committed suicide.
17. Coinsider, a precocious crypto Youtuber, did warn LUNA about its Ponzi-like structure.
18. Some viewers berate him, but not many viewed his channel before the unpegging.

19. And now, he is the oracle that everyone wishes that they had listened to or discovered.
20. Reclining on the carpet like a pregnant log of wood, my brother asked if I invested much.
21. I said I bought one share (to study) at $109 and when it dropped to $34 dollars, I bought another share.
22. And when it went to $2, I bought 10 more, etc. and when it went down to $.008, I bought $140 more, and then Crypto.com delisted LUNA and UST from its exchange.
23. Everyone else follows.
24. My investment in LUNA in limbo.
25. Lunatics lost $20 mil, $1.6 mil, $57K, $10K, but the maximum amount I lost: $500, which is pocket change for some people.
26. I reasoned if they were able to reverse it, maybe I can buy my mother the house she always dreamed of.
27. I reasoned it was like throwing my left breast into a black hole.
28. Most likely it would never come back, but if there is a chance that $500 could become a couple million, why not take that chance?
29. After all, a $100 investment in Shiba Inu, a year ago on its first day (August 1st, 2020), was worth over $3 million.
30. My brother said he put all of his money in Redbox.
31. He reasoned that with Netflix going supremely downhill, with viewers and subscribers shifting to other venues, Redbox seems like a baby that needs to be burped by his investment.
32. Meanwhile, my partner is in Lafayette moving and packing and breaking down things in order to end her lease.

33. She is utterly exhausted, looking like me when I had AFib and even after cardioversion converted me back to normal sinus rhythm, I still looked like a woman who climbed 70 stairs every five minutes.
34. My brother has extraordinary reasoning skills.

THURSDAY MAY 12, 2022

1. While waiting for my brother to collect me, I folded his laundry.
2. He wears the same things over and over: striped boxers, black shirts, and thin nylon-like pants.
3. His clothes have swelled and enlarged to match his recent expansion: weight gain.
4. I worry all the time about his heart.
5. Beating beneath his shirt with intense arrhythmia.
6. His face, hands, and legs swelled from his heart being unable to eliminate fluid from his body.
7. He loves fresh-squeezed orange juice, chips dipped in salsa, whole chicken dipped in lime, salt, and pepper.
8. My brother surprised me by telling me that his Uber passenger in North Liberty had held his time hostage and that he won't be able to take me to my doctor's appointment.
9. Sitting in an Uber car with an Uber driver named David, I think: the intense smell of sweat and mildew.
10. I stopped breathing in his car and think about my brother who doesn't drink coffee, but reheated already brewed coffee into all four of his coffee flasks so that his car smelled wonderful for his passengers.
11. My brother takes the extra steps and it makes all the difference for those who sit in his passenger seat.
12. He did make it in time to collect me after the appointment.
13. My best friend, AR, and my sweetheart, J, both Zoomed in to be with me.
14. After kibitzing on the tenderness exhibited between us digitally, the doctor asked if I had HIV.

15. Understanding the underlining message of prejudice and casual ignorance, I said boldly, "No."
16. I may have a lot of ailments, but HIV isn't one of them.
17. The doctor ordered many tests: to check my ferritin and iron levels, my NT-proBNP, my sedimentation rate, erythrocyte, hemoglobin, eosinophil %, and even my vitamin B12 level and my red blood cell distribution width.
18. Meanwhile, in my brother's car, we headed to my youngest sister's place, where I wait for her meeting to end.
19. She drove me to the grocery store in her top-down convertible.
20. The sun was bleating strong and so was the wave of heat.
21. We got my brother Cuties mandarins, popsicles, and different kinds of pre-cut fruit.
22. He loves oranges, I tell my youngest sister.
23. Years ago, when he landed in the ER, she drove to Missouri to be with him and clean out his semi.
24. There were so many orange peels, she exclaimed in reminiscence.
25. When I climbed downstairs to refill my water glasses, I noticed that my brother had washed my dirty dishes and his as well.

FRIDAY MAY 13, 2022

1. After my brother eats a full meal, he reclines on the carpet in the living room.
2. It pains me each time he does so.
3. I always want to say something, but if I do, he may feel self-conscious and I may not see him at all.
4. Even if I am just a hallway across from his bedroom.
5. It is a terrible habit that exacerbates his acid reflux situation.
6. Everything can't be resolved with 40mg pantoprazole tablets.
7. I keep my mouth shut so I could spend more time with him.
8. My brother has a way of expressing a distaste or dislike for something that others do by disappearing into the unknown.
9. It may be months before I see him emerging out of his bedroom.
10. And time isn't on his side and for sure not on mine.
11. My blood work came back and now I know why I have been exhausted, sleeping 14 hours a day for two weeks straight.
12. At 7:39, my brother texted a photo of his Nissan.
13. Some drunk college student egged his car.
14. My sister asked, "Were u in the car?"
15. He was.
16. Always quick on her feet, my sister added, "Eggs r getting $$, they can't keep up for long."
17. Some organic eggs at Hy-vee are $6.99 for a dozen.
18. My brother group-texted at 9:13 am to share a picture of Bruce Teague, the Iowa City mayor at-large.
19. He Ubered him and his mother to Davenport.

20. It's an hour Uber ride in which afterward, his mother tipped him $20.
21. The mayor looked like a body builder.
22. "He was my customer this morning," my brother texted.
23. My sister suggested, "Did u tell him about the drunk college population egging ppls car that he needs to address as a mayor at large of iowa city?"
24. "I got his email address" was all my brother texted back.
25. Meanwhile, the doctor called me to tell me about my results.
26. I learned that my troponin level is abnormally high and that I have heart failure.
27. As I was celebrating the virtue of dying young, my mother called.
28. To tell me about BlackRock, who manages about $10 trillion worth of other people's money.
29. It was rumored that they and Citadel joint-attacked Terraform Labs, which led at least 20 people to commit suicide after the Ponzi scheme pegged UST and LUNA fiasco.
30. While I type this, I can hear my brother taking deep breaths in his midday/late evening sleep.
31. It's heartening for two siblings with similar heart failure to find comfort in each other's company.

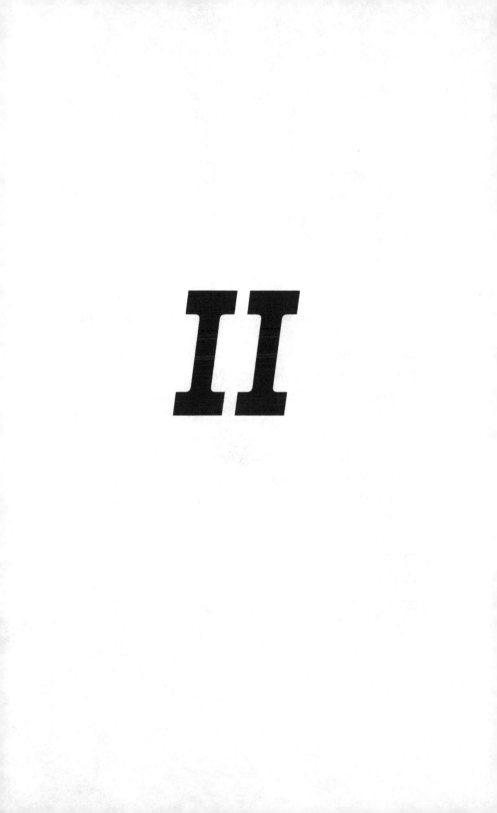

I ALWAYS CRAVE A SMALL QUIET DEATH, GENERATIONAL SUICIDE WITHIN MY SMALL NUCLEAR FAMILY

1. My father passing away
2. My mother too,
3. Following immediately
4. My brother and not too soon
5. After
6. Within 12 hours
7. Me
8. I think about the woman with a belittled imagination
9. The woman in me
10. Who could not foresee
11. The beauty in the insubstantial
12. The sorrow in the infinite
13. I think
14. I am ready for
15. That which I am not ready for
16. I think I am that clover
17. Hovering
18. In the dark
19. That glove that
20. Won't fit anyone
21. That dove that
22. Was shot down by
23. A mini 14

THERE IS THIS THING ABOUT WANTING EVERY-THING AT ONCE IN CELSIUS, THERE IS THIS THING WITH THE WEATHER

1. Outside the forest is playing the xylophone
2. The mallets are sporadic rainwater
3. Clung to the tips of leaves in wild bursts
4. Onto the cedar trees as two women in love
5. Weave their fingers into a basket of an afternoon
6. When snow walks her sister, the wind, home
7. From middle school — the dark road that leads to nowhere
8. Awaits her children like an anxious mother
9. When I take apart the snow globe
10. To change snow into a thunderstorm
11. A xenophobe into a xylophone

I MIS-MEASURE YOUR SILENCE FOR *TELEPATHY* & YOUR SADNESS FOR *EMPATHY*

1. I am no saint tasting your nerve impulses,[1]
2. The sound of your chair
3. Creaking leads me to a conjunction on the side of the road
4. Each word goes inside their sovereign domain
5. Each word there is a *path*
6. Just as I reach my hand out to touch you
7. You return to sand
8. I am forced to be *resilient*
9. When all I want to do is give up *hope*

1 Prompt: Eat something inedible and write a poem about it

YOU ARE NOT A LOAF OF BREAD THAT THE
NIGHT MUST FORGIVE IN ORDER TO BE
VIOLENT

1. a spoon
2. is a boat
3. i stuff into
4. my body

I'M GOING TO HOLD YOUR MONEY HOSTAGE IF YOU ARE NOT NICE TO ME & ACCOMMODATIONS ARE 2X $$ DURING X-MAS[2]

1. This is canh chua shrimp &
2. Mực [hấp hành gừng]
3. It's pretty beat up
4. And, I don't know what national security mortgage is
5. I am over bleeding
6. About 1/2 cup of menstrual blood every half an hour
7. They will overnight it
8. Remotely
9. That's the day I close
10. How is your heart?
11. Are you watching? We cancel each other out of internet
12. Disregard silver earbuds
13. They usually sleep downstairs

---

2 Prompt: A poem using text messages sent to a family

IF YOU MUST BEG, DO NOT WEAR THE SAME
GARMENT AS THE FUTURE

1. Tears carry their wallet in an almond-shaped purse
2. At   the metro   a distraught woman tries to pay
3. Her ticket to Coney Island (her *Phú Quốc*, *my pocket*
4. *change)*   by sobbing \
5. When   I open   their purse, inside: happiness is
   holding
6. a large umbrella
7. The color of despair   the shape of presage
8. &   laughing

LICK MY EYELID BEFORE YOU GO, SAY YOUR
ORGANS ARE LONELY, RUB MY HIP
STUDIOUSLY, COMB MY HAIR NOW TO AVOID
PATROL, HAVE MY LIVER FOR LIFE

1. April is a metropolitan of rain
2. Fall and February   are lodged
3. In the throat   of   Pisces
4. Take   me   to your doorstep
5. Then   suffocate   me. The doorbell works really well
6. Correct me if I find my lover succumbing to one
   thousand
7. Grams of salt   three fistfuls   of sugar and one clover
8. Wait for it *Ardor* while I whisper *Inaudible.*

THE ECONOMY OF YOUR DESIRE HAS ENTERED
THE ICE AGE OVERNIGHT, FROZEN LAKES OF
DESPAIR, IT WILL TAKE FOREVER TO THAW
OUT YOUR HAIR, EXOGENOUS ZONES, THE
EVERGLADES OF YOUR TONGUE & FINGER
MORTGAGES, THE UNEMPLOYMENT BENEFITS
OF OUR KISSES HAVE PLUNGED INTO 26
MILLION, THERE ARE BILLIONS OF STIMULA-
TION, BUT NONE COULD GET THE DICK HARD,
ENOUGH TO KICK THE DEPRESSION AWAY

1. I am starving tens and thousands
2. Of your pleasure points
3. There is intimacy famine of biblical scope
4. Amongst the transit workers of
5. Your sex drive & our therapists tell me
6. It's a good time to homeschool your nipples
7. It's a good time to social distance
8. The bank account of today from yesterday
9. It's a good time to reopen the masturbation
10. Of defeatism and melancholy
11. It's a good time to give inadequate aids
12. To your broken toes, your misguided hormones
13. It's a good time to budget constraint
14. The lingerie of the pandemic
15. I want to kiss the global economy away
16. I want this nightmare to be over
17. I want the freedom to walk the white
18. Arctic bears of your warmth, your devotion,
19. Your ardent disposition, your penchant for
20. Sympathy and altruism down
21. The avenues of our bedsheets

22. The color of this rice paddy and lay your
23. Soft mouth against the flesh of my atrophy

MY ROOT IS NOT A MIRROR, WHICH HAS THE FACE OF GLASS, MY ROOT ISN'T AN ORCHID, NOT WATERED IN A WEEK

1. Or [Over the weekend]
2. The light floating in from its insular root
3. Is a jellyfish [con sứa]
4. Con sứa hollowed out
5. By the mirror of her distance
6. I come forward
7. Wearing a [verdant : màu xanh lá]
8. Short-sleeve shirt
9. My root is, thus, then
10. A whenever, a however, a nowhere-ever
11. [I doubt I have loved you]
12. In this refracted soil
13. [I doubt you could wear my voice]
14. Branching through your ethnic
15. điểm khởi đầu

I CAN'T HURRY TIME FOR YOU OR TIE IT TO A DOOR KNOB TO STRETCH IT OUT LIKE A RUBBER BAND TO ONE'S TONGUE OR TO PLACE IT ON A PLATTER OF SMOKE

1. I can't rush time out of the door as I would
2. With a man who sells knives door to door
3. I can't even ask time to tie his shoelaces faster
4. Or to come to my funeral a day early
5. I can't ask time to climb over those hills and valleys
6. I called your voluptuous body
7. Wearing tennis shoes I call the internet
8. While you age slowly across several millennia
9. I can't beg time to sit on a pressure cooker
10. So that his bones would break apart fastest
11. So that there would be more boiling points
12. In my desire or my small autumn for you
13. I can't gallop time through the four corners
14. Of my bedsheet just so that I could make the bed
15. Of my affection for you with the speed of light
16. I can't pound time to get the hell out of here
17. To sprint, hasten, dash, dive, stampede the hour,
18. The second, the tempo, the pulse, the rhythm,
19. The meter, the cadence,
20. The ambience, the music of my exquisite
21. Breath which lies between your mouth
22. & my second tongue, timelessness
23. I now hold time in my bosom and strokes his
24. Hair and tell him to leave his five o'clock shadow
25. On the driveway of my watch's face
26. While I lean in to kiss an ardor which
27. Has become my new time machine

EVERY DRESS IS A SIMILE

1. Every breath is a metaphor
2. Every smile is a symbol
3. Every finger is a personification
4. Every gaze is a hyperbole
5. Every hunt is an alliteration
6. Every exaggeration is an onomatopoeia
7. Every despair is an idiom
8. Every speaker is an imagery

THE WOMAN I LOVE HAS ENDLESS COMPAS-
SION FOR ME YET IN THE MIDDLE OF THE
NIGHT I LEFT HER & LIFE FOR DEATH

1. There was infinite discord in my soul
2. Infinite conjunction of pain
3. &, blissfully, so blissfully I hung my neck
4. From a modern-day cypress
5. & the young emboldened leaves
6. Not mulched in their fortuitous youth
7. Screamed in tumultuous calamity
8. From their verdant height
9. Had confused me for a dying leaf
10. Had waited so patiently for me
11. Not to exfoliate from a branch in life
12. When my neck broke into two
13. In response to the weight of gravity
14. They thought an inner twig had separated
15. A blade of photosynthesis from
16. An artery of time
17. I suppose time could take
18. A long walk with me
19. By the river of death
20. I suppose it is never
21. Too late to hold life's hand
22. Briefly while the sun comes
23. Down from that mountain
24. Before letting her go
25. Into a city designed for pulsing

SNOW WHITE PAINTED HER LIPS WITH MY
SPERM & IF THE SEA IS HER MIRROR & MY
BELLY IS HER SKY IN WHICH YOUR OIL
RECOILS, YOUR COCOA BUTTER HOVERS, YOUR
PIGMENT MY CUPID'S BOW

1. You give plutonic birth to death
2. Fading heavily in your graveyard
3. The wars, the hungers, the infant birth defects
4. I travel the night in my labyrinth, chthonic nightgown
5. I wilt the widows
6. I wither the orphans
7. Demeter wandering above like deistic priests
8. Her daughter revolutionizes my personal
9. Diary of genocide
10. Wheat and winter
11. Calories and protean proteins
12. Diploid grass mourning the Bronte sisters in the wind

FROM THIS CENTURY BOUND BY THE META-BOLIC FORCE OF WASTE I CRY INTO INFINITY, CAKING GLASS WITH DEBRIS, THIS NIVAL RED HEMOGLOBIN SPEAKING

1. Octopus seeks immobility
2. By extending its shattered
3. Tentacles of cannon and lurch
4. Light is debris
5. Soft bodice
6. Beaklike violence
7. The plural form[3]
8. Of mother and child
9. Of sister and young brother
10. Made singular by
11. Adverse extinction
12. Its internal shell
13. Gravity the unsurmountable
14. The plant, the air
15. The fire
16. In triangulated
17. Sea turtles & tumbleweeds

3 Stanley Forman's "Woman Falling From Fire Escape" 1975

WOULD YOU MONETIZE HAIR PULLING?

1. White privilege
2. White fragility
3. Denying oppression
4. "We are losing our jokes"
5. Black lungs
6. Coal mines
7. Slavery the most violent form of violence
8. Business license
9. Bag clutching license
10. Being shot (Andy Warhol)
11. Be yourself license
12. "Against Our Will"
13. "Emmitt Till"
14. Fantasy
15. Would you like to monetize hair pulling?

HOLDING MY FACE AGAINST THE FLASK MY LOVER CAULKS MY BODY TO THE BATHROOM DOOR

1. So, I wouldn't leave the quarantine zone for *gelato*
2. Ridges & obituary *falling* from virus debris in Italy
3. Migrant memory as waterproof *sealant* for our past
4. For I am *not* silicon — just cracks in   between *me*   &   *masonry*
5. I tread with *force*, waiting to *copulate* with your *budgerigar*
6. I forgive you if it *mimics* my human *voice* back to me
7. I forgive what I couldn't *debilitate*
8. *Flasks, masks, 793 dead bodies* strolling
9. down the streets military style
10. Death *boldly* declares this year is *his* year

IN THE YEAR AND ERA OF OUR QUARAN-
TINE YOUR TEARS WANDER THE VACANT
STREETS AT NIGHT, ONE FLUVIAL WET FOOT-
STEP AT A TIME DESOLATE & FORGIVING &
NOT UNIFORMED BEFORE ARRIVING TO THE
ATRIUM OF MY BREATH
for Bree Cameron

1. Though aware of each other's existence
2. I know your tears & mine never met
3. Never walk the same forgotten bridge, the same boulevard,
4. the same graveyard, the same church, the same coffee shop, the same
5. restaurant, the same bar, the same telephone booth, the same tree
6. Until all souls, old and young, and their cluttered, cancellable contents
7. are forced indoors
8. But, now, just yesterday your tears fall from their bewildering height
9. Onto my digital sleeves in broad daylight
10. Soaking the cities of my enemy, flooding the crumpled
11. bodies of old electronic
12. newspapers, sedating an army of words
13. & images as they float downstream
14. in the digital stream towards their untimely deaths
15. As you introduced yourself to me for the very first time
16. If your tears & my tears could hold each other's hands
17. While wandering quietly & soundlessly through

18. the different Instagram *corridors* as
19. we intimately   share the history of our melancholy, our demoralizing
20. lives before the Great Flood, the *1918 Flu Pandemic*, before the era
21. of the *Me Too Movement*, before the Great Depression
22. If *your* tears & *my* tears could fall asleep *together* on this *pillow* & its
23. devastatingly beautiful *pillowcase* called *poetry*
24. Our tears could come home after many years of
25. meaningless, futile travels, get on
26. their pluvial knees to sink and soak until
27. they are free of their human debris
28. Wouldn't that be so awesome, Bree?

MY LEFT BREAST HAS NOT BEEN ABLE TO
SLEEP ON A HOT SUMMER DAY WITH HER
NIPPLE TURNED TOWARDS THE CADILLAC

1. The daylight savings thing
2. made my bladder too active
3. I self-quarantine *self-quarantine*
4. In my twenties
5. I was a birch tree
6. My sexuality was thin bark
7. grown predominantly on the northern
8. province of my psyche
9. & later I told King Solomon to cut
10. the baby in halves —
11. half for him half for me
12. nothing for the mothers
13. My hair was full &&& dark & exquisite
14. & I fucked anything that was made of limestone
15. I even fucked some taro roots & if I am honest

INFINITY IS A CLOCK WITH DREAMS & WITH NO FORBEARANCE & NO LENIENCY &, I, WHO KNOWS THE LAW OF LAMENTING SO WELL, MOVE THE OCEAN INDOORS AND CLOSE THE CURTAINS — OF COURSE, OF COURSE — THEY ARE SYLPH BEINGS ANCHORED BY DEVASTATION & LUMINESCENCE

1. Each raindrop is a body of words
2. Clothed in distillation & synchronicity
3. You are synthetic & I am fabric
4. Worn just yesterday before
5. I am so desolate
6. So wanting your lettuce romaine
7. Over olive oil from the middle
8. Of the sea and east of your apex
9. Pinnacle of displeasure
10. You give me so much pleasure
11. Of diversion & I, who does not
12. Know better, confuse it
13. For an inversion of shame
14. Take me to your house of
15. Words where your piano
16. Makes love to me by
17. Crushing me to the bottom
18. Of an office drawer
19. In the morning you are sweeping
20. Tears into a dust pan

IN LIFE I AM LED TO NOWHERE BY THE LEFT
HAND OF YOUR HOPE & IN DEATH I IMAGINE
ALL THE POSSIBILITIES: YOU GETTING INTO A
HEAD-ON COLLISION WITH DESTINY & YOUR
SEMI JACK-KNIFED BY THE INSECURITIES AND
DOUBTS THAT LED US ASTRAY

1. Even with all the broken glasses
2. The shattered windshield
3. Just last night
4. You are simply a tea kettle
5. Pulled over by the ambulance
6. Of importance, imbalance, remorse
7. You pull me into your arms
8. &, I hiss and I steam
9. You always lead me
10. To a boiling point
11. At exactly 212 degrees Fahrenheit
12. While you murmur
13. Heart disease, coumadin, turmoil

MY BABY IS IN MY BED & SEXY & MY BABY,
WHOSE TIT IS EVERGREEN, IS HICCUPING ON
MY STOVE WHILE I AM RAINING RADISH INTO
YOUR SKI BOOT & IT'S YESTERDAY'S AFTER-
NOON WHILE HER ORANGE FEATHER IS BOUND
BY RUBBER NEAR A FLORAL OF SOYBEANS[4]

1. My baby
2. is sleeping
3. in a grave in
4. yellow Tunisia.
5. *You were blue*, she announced,
6. when I roll around
7. In a crate of soil.
8. The earth is twisted
9. with forgotten roots.
10. I crawl through fog
11. baked by mist, cough
12. a plate of snow,
13. It's never too late.
14. While the earth
15. heaves a lake
16. of avifauna,
17. time pulls my
18. hair gently
19. into a time machine.

4 Lines from Adrienne Herr & from page 5 of Shira Erlichman's *Odes to Lithium*

I WANT YOUR BRIEF ESCARPMENT HIGH-LIGHTING A YOUTHFUL PERFECTION, ITS DAILY TASK, AND I WANT A DOOR TO EMBODY MY SPIRITUAL BOTTOM

1. there awaits a nipple
2. divided by loneliness
3. after screen off, wishfully
4. small portions of astronomy
5. guided by an ambushed
6. desire

1. 9, 1, 1, forlorn as a zenith
2. by sea silhouette filming
3. nine lives, you.
4. for nadir:
5. a mirror of yearning,
6. or warm icebergs?

1. Now
2. i have lived as a horse,
3. pulling the nipple's taut interiority, hey
4. the earth is still round
5. what you don't see you can't forgive
6. without the edge knowing

I GAZE AT MY NONSELF, KNOWING THAT I
HAVEN'T EXISTED YET, BUT IN YOU MY OTHER
SELF REVEALS ITS METAL AMALGAM, IT
REVEALS THAT I AM NOT YOU, I AM A
DISTORTED FRAGMENT OF SOMETHING SOFT
IN THE PERIPHERY

1. The antidote to a mirror
2. Is a mirror
3. That gazes not back at me after I cease to exist
4. It gazes to see if I cease to exist,
5. Existence will have a full mouth and a translucent face
6. It doesn't seize nor oppress itself
7. Completely in the reflective memory of a mirror
8. Mirror, Mirror
9. Prior to your mirrorless anecdote
10. I name my daughter after you
11. I call her
12. Self

I TOOK A NAP ON AN ELECTRIC CHAIR AND
CONFUSED IT FOR A FLOCK OF PRIVATE ELEC-
TROCUTION AS SUCH THERE IS A DEER IN MY
RED EARTH PAST, BOWING HER HEAD SIMI-
LARLY TO A BLACK AND WHITE ÁO DÀI

1. There comes a sorrow
2. Wider than two extrajudicial hipbones of
3. Pre-gravid women in their late twenties
4. The chair was a wire, an electrical wire
5. That stretches between 1979 to 2022
6. It stretches its cliffhanging voltage
7. From my rebirth to my birth
8. From Đồng Nai Province to Iowa City
9. Outside, Mother Superior
10. Chews on her Indo-European roots
11. Like summer grass across that clearing
12. Indecent, it may seem
13. To compare religion to whale and rhinoceros bones
14. To compare my Indo-China bath
15. As a bird — for distorting
16. A mid-flight resting
17. On an electrical wire
18. For capital punishment

THOSE MORAL-HARDENED REPUBLICANS
WITH THEIR RED NOSES PRESSED AGAINST THE
SILK SCREEN OF DEMOCRACY, RODE THOSE
MACHINE GUNS AND SMOKE GRENADES INTO
THE CAPITAL, I AM FOREVER CALIFORNIA
REPUBLIC LIKE REDWOOD BURNING HER
SEQUOIA HEART BEATS INTO THAT QUIET CITY
OF FIRE AND FOG

1. Those winter days deployed by the Senate
2. Left tear gas falling from your bruised, astringent
   cheeks
3. Snow White dressed like one of the seven dwarves
4. I am afraid that that French kiss
5. The soldier of one century left on my left temple
6. At mid-daylight has deserted
7. Impaling me between the anachronistic limousine of
   the past
8. And the coeval solar motorcar of the abiogenic future
9. As such your red star and macerated gaze
10. Sat like a pair of unworn blue jeans on that
    democratic
11. Thighs which shuffled your memory of the Civil War
12. Like a deck of poker face cards on this Thursday table
13. Last night, I ate a tomato sliced into quadrants
14. Of beehive and pastoral lingering. I sprinkled salt
15. And tasted one nightshade family — a potato perhaps
    —
16. An eggplant in an afterthought — being deathly
    vulgar
17. With my glossa: capsicum peppers, jimson weed,
    henbane

18. These hostile plant concubines spread their malevolent
19. Seeds and pungent thighs eyrie
20. Simply to poison me into a shade which isn't a nightshade

JEAN-MICHEL BASQUIAT BORROWS MY FACE
FOR *READY PLAYER ONE*, HOW EAGER, HOW
WILLING HALLIDAY'S DEATH SERVED MY SIMU-
LATED ARCHIVE WHILE MY MEMORY HIDES
OUT IN A SORRENTO NIGHTCLUB, WHILE
DESTINY EXISTS IN PARZIVAL DRIVING BACK-
WARDS INTO SPACE MEANWHILE NICOLAS
CAGE

1. Becomes
2. Two-faced
3. In Las Vegas
4. Hairy chest like a roof made of
5. Black grass, black hay
6. Your
7. Poor money management
8. Your bald eyebrows
9. Spreading eagle on my television screen
10. The first woman I ever loved
11. Thought you were so sexy
12. She was Chinese

MY FATHER SEPARATES THE THEME OF
UNHAPPINESS FROM MY LIFE, HE SEPARATES
THE INTOLERANCE FROM THE VIOLENCE,
WISDOM FROM INDECISION, BALANCE FROM
SCALE, EYES FROM COG, HE

1. Takes my rabbit from
2. A woman who claims the soft
3. Bunny is hers
4. The oracle takes my father's hands and tells him
5. "Son, Be King Solomon —
6. Split that rabbit into two"
7. His ears I love the most
8. For I could use them to
9. Listen to its dorsiflexors all day
10. Your mollusk is my husk
11. Metaphorically speaking not
12. Our young tedious date on Gastropoda
13. When we have sex, we fuck in our own separate adobe
14. Your grandparent's condo terrestrially pulmonated
    above mine
15. Freshwater is how I seduce off Tinder
16. On Tinder, you are my rebirth

POEM FROM THE POINT OF VIEW OF A BAT &
POEM FROM THE POINT OF VIEW OF A
BUTTERFLY & POEM THAT ABDUCTS APATHY
FROM ICE POSEIDON

1. His unstated splendor
2. His magnificent lethargy
3. His exquisite masculinity
4. Can't be echolocated
5. Can't echo off my cave
6. But, like a blind Tiresias
7. I crave what I cannot see
8. Can darkness detect what I cannot decree?
9. Can his inevitable curls
10. Murmur this point of view?
11. My wings could be that tree
12. Covet me in residuum
13. If my brother is Abel?
14. Cain's sorrow is that he is forced
15. To compete with the invisible
16. I bleed in whetted soil
17. Fluttering over what should not be biblical

I PLACE YOUR HEAD INTO THE MACHINERY OF MY SOLITUDE & PRAY DAY AND NIGHT FOR THE RAZOR BLADES OF INTELLECT TO SHAVE MY ARMPIT HAIRS

1. I relish what has been taken
2. For sky, for lightning, for contained
3. Burns — I relish
4. My place in your arms' armory
5. And, when I shave my legs
6. I tell you the hair casualties
7. Are diminutive
8. Small, forgotten like water
9. Like snow receding
10. From the poignant nipple
11. Of that Toyoko mountain

NOT WISHING TO END MY LIFE IN A WELL I HAVE MEASURED MY ANENCEPHALIC APPETITE WITH AN INFLECTION LACED IN AVADAVAT'S FEATHER

1. The nascent ambush
2. Ambulates around my eye duct
3. Quack for the ophthalmological canal
4. Shaft moving one pipeline in body, in audio
5. I face my invisibility by fluttering
6. My heart — its music above the empyrean sky
7. Its lower chamber without trachea,
8. Without inlet, without
9. You dressed for my indecipherable ambush
10. I fall from your fingertip one piano cord
11. Each hammer depressed, each soundboard three pedals
12. Away from that rash
13. A flower polished by your voice climbing out of
14. A shaft — oil, water, gas
15. My suicide is ambient light for those
16. Who rides the nocturnal sky with a knife
17. Whetted for politics, for self, for resistance

MY YELLOW HEART WITHERS, CATALOGUING ITS LEMONY GRANITE WHILE YOU UNCANNED MY TOMATO SAUCE

1. My midnight: soft
2. You're bread. You're diameter.
3. You disquieted my opaque reflection
4. Like a shuttlecock: predator,
5. The pedophile of daylight
6. Distorted alongside the unsettling evening
7. You face
8. The monsoon — the telescope of my lost rope
9. You spiral inside my nightmare —
10. You're my viscera
11. My Bui Vien Street
12. Over, over deepening intestines
13. Hotspot for hitchhikers
14. I trekked down 4,344 streets
15. Half of my eyes expecting fire & smoke
16. I stylize your middle name
17. With beetle leaves
18. Purple and crimson
19. Nucleus
20. And, incarcerated
21. And, as a prefix
22. Respond by crying

THE SUICIDAL RAIN CLIMBS THE LAMPPOSTS, DESCENDS THE ASPHALT, AND SOMEHOW IT WAS ALL OF MY FAULT, IT WAS ALL MY FAULT

1. The suicidal rain
2. Is the refrain in my outer coast
3. It's the sea
4. It's the rooster in a corncob
5. The suicidal rain
6. Memorizes my name
7. Memorizes my refrain
8. Memorizes its mainframe
9. The suicidal rain
10. Drains my blood
11. Oscillating all my French shutters in its euthanistic tongue
12. This suicidal rain
13. Retrains my umbilical oboe
14. So it is a noose
15. In my cervical discord
16. Oh, this suicidal rain
17. Flashing
18. Flooding
19. Flooring
20. A circle
21. Within this suicidal infinity
22. Within this dumfounded disharmony
23. Oh, this suicidal rain

MY DUSKY SOUL SOILED IN GLOOMY NARRA-
TIVE WHILE I ATE THE BLEACHED
CAULIFLOWER OF MY ADVERSARY, MY
SERFOM, MY INFANT, MY DREAMSCAPE

1. Back arched, moon falling
2. Whisper into my arboreal gloom, hovering
3. Clusters of canine, holy Harriet Tubman
4. My new boxer — a boat, its arrow of velocity in me
5. Cloud wizards, shivers of white
6. Gathering sound while my silhouette survives
7. Pregnant, I vomit slavery while my son collects marijuana into his mouth
8. He flings high, my form reserves its own personal echo in its own cowbell
9. If the cloud could behave well in a zombie film, his performance/acting has such resemblance
10. To the winter months; curtains and scythe mimic each other's tongues.
11. In the distance, my memory of independence
12. Meanwhile, he farted black clouds while my child followed me into a well as I held the face of bondage across from this reform
13. Legs above estate, acres of sinecure

TENDERGRASS WILTED IN POWER & IDENTITY, WITHERED IN WINDSHIELDED WINDFLOWERS, WINDBURNED BY SENSUAL DETAILS OF THYME

1. Tenderness is not overrated — our intimacy soft as hay butter
2. Flecks of emptiness — how I have aged, luminescently
3. Pulling my grandmother from earth — her inmate is snake
4. I stand between footstep + glance
5. It strikes me as military — the edge crowded by citrus flamingos
6. Eyes hovering like post autumn equinox, drone view of his consent for my pending widowhood
7. Taut, razored sharp, war bitten, not yet poison
8. My prison is Eve's virtue weaved intellectually in Adam's surgical sin
9. Her cheekbones, ablaze by the desiccated wind, grows smaller + smaller
10. Pungent by symmetry, pungent by some sharp ocular pedigree
11. Umbilical grass laced + relaced in serenity
12. I place my nuptial hand over the fabric of my sweater, the color of floating predatory birds
13. Marriage that can't fly — won't fly without the bovine twisted in the divine
14. Murmurs the avian Prometheus dressed in black and white

ABOUT THE AUTHOR

VI KHI NAO was chosen as the 2022 Lambda Literary Award Winner of the Jim Duggins, PhD Outstanding Mid-Career Novelist Prize. She is the author of 17 books, including: *A Brief Alphabet of Torture: Stories*, which won FC2's 2016 Ronald Sukenick Innovative Fiction Prize; the novels *Fish in Exile* (Coffee House Press, 2016) and *Swimming with Dead Stars* (The University of Alabama Press, 2022); and the poetry collection *The Old Philosopher* (Nightboat Books, 2016), which won the 2014 Nightboat Poetry Prize. Her work includes poetry, fiction, nonfiction, chapbooks, films, plays, cross-genre writing, media art, and collaboration.

VIKHINAO.COM